ARCTIC

SCANDINAVIA

EAST
AND
SOUTH
EUROPE

COMMONWEALTH OF
INDEPENDENT STATES

THE
MIDDLE
EAST

CHINA AND ITS
NEIGHBOURS

INDIA AND ITS
NEIGHBOURS

AFRICA

TROPIC OF CAPRICORN

AUSTRALIA AND
SOUTH EAST ASIA

THE ANTARCTIC

Contents

Published in Great Britain by World International Publishing Ltd.,
an Egmont Company, Egmont House, PO Box 111,
Great Ducie Street, Manchester M60 3BL.
Printed in Singapore.
ISBN 0-7498-1730-5

This edition specially produced for
Ted Smart, Guardian House, Borough Road,
Godalming, Surrey GU7 2AE

My First
Atlas

with lift-the-flap
surprises

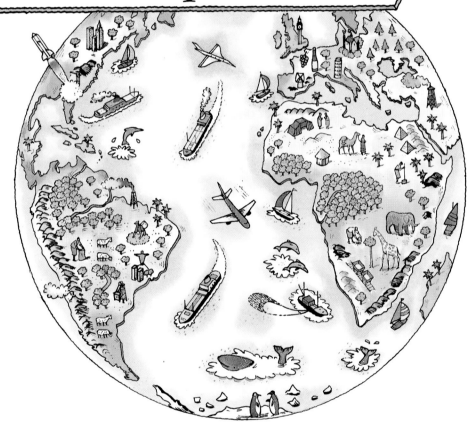

illustrated by Colin King

text by Chris Oxlade and Anita Ganeri
designed by Ian Butterworth

TED SMART

North America

North America is the third largest continent. It stretches from the hot deserts of Mexico in the south to the Arctic Circle in the north. Greenland is covered in thick ice. Lake Superior is one of the five Great Lakes. It is the world's largest freshwater lake. The Grand Canyon, in the United States, is the world's largest canyon.

This is where North America is on the globe.

When the time in London is 9 o'clock in the morning…

…it is 4 o'clock in the morning in New York, United States.

KEY TO SYMBOLS USED	
Mountains	
Forests	
Deserts	
Grassland	
Ice and snow	
★ Capital city	

Moose
Moose live in Canada. They are the largest deer. Their antlers can measure 2 metres across (6 feet).

North American Indians

Golden Gate Bridge
This famous bridge is in San Francisco. It is 1,280 metres long (4,200 feet).

Mexico flag

UNITED STATES
(Alaska)

• Anchorage

Vancouver

• Seattle

Pacific Ocean

Sierra Nevada

San Francisco

Las Vegas

Los Angeles •

Grand Canyon

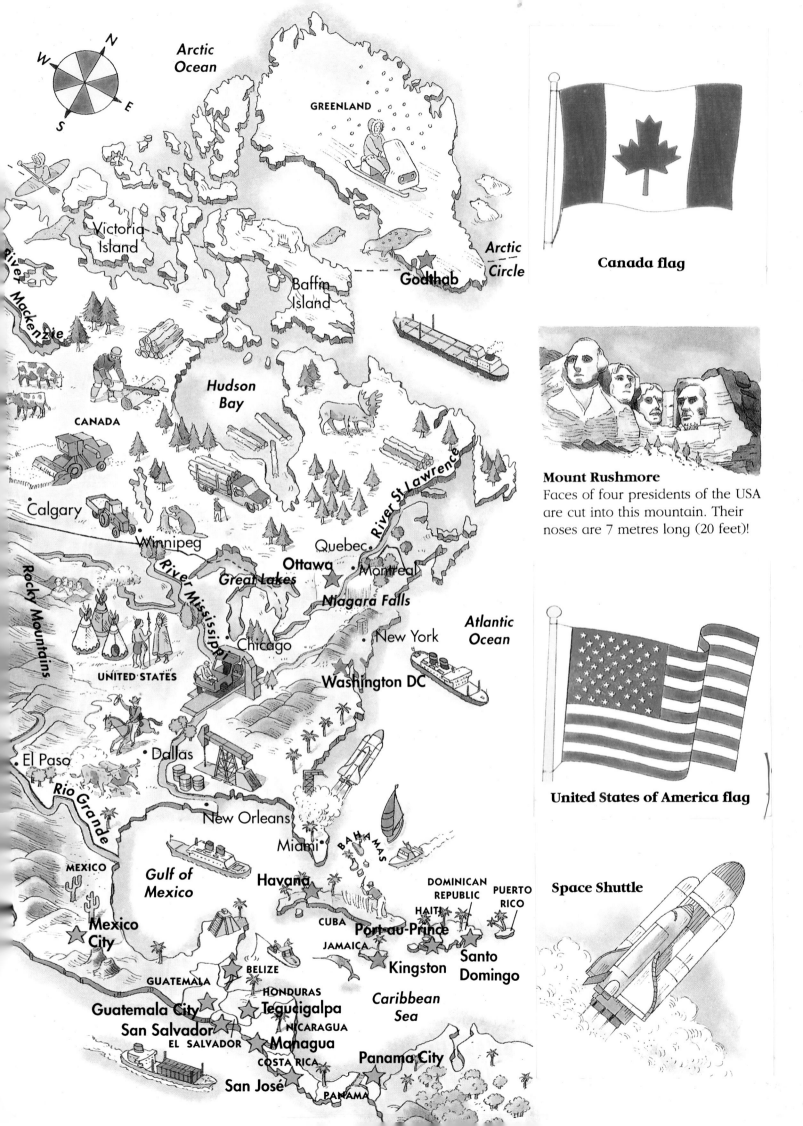

Canada flag

Mount Rushmore
Faces of four presidents of the USA are cut into this mountain. Their noses are 7 metres long (20 feet)!

United States of America flag

Space Shuttle

Arctic Ocean

GREENLAND

Victoria Island

River Mackenzie

Arctic Circle

Baffin Island

Godthab

Hudson Bay

CANADA

Calgary

Winnipeg

River St Lawrence

Quebec

Ottawa

Montreal

Great Lakes

Niagara Falls

Rocky Mountains

River Mississippi

Chicago

New York

Atlantic Ocean

UNITED STATES

Washington DC

El Paso

Dallas

Rio Grande

New Orleans

Miami

BAHAMAS

MEXICO

Gulf of Mexico

Havana

DOMINICAN REPUBLIC

PUERTO RICO

HAITI

Mexico City

CUBA

Port-au-Prince

JAMAICA

Santo Domingo

Kingston

BELIZE

GUATEMALA

HONDURAS

Caribbean Sea

Guatemala City

Tegucigalpa

San Salvador

EL SALVADOR

NICARAGUA

Managua

Panama City

COSTA RICA

San José

PANAMA

7

South America

South America is linked to North America by a thin strip of land. The River Amazon flows through the huge Amazon Rainforest. The river is 6,440 kilometres long (4,000 miles) and is the second longest river in the world. The Andes Mountains stretch down the west side of South America.

This is where South America is on the globe.

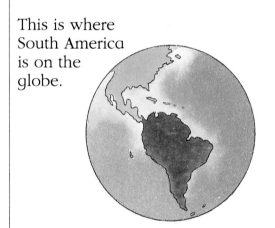

When the time in London is 9 o'clock in the morning…

…it is 5 o'clock in the morning in Brasilia, Brazil.

KEY TO SYMBOLS USED

Mountains	
Deserts	
Grassland	
Tropical forests	
★	Capital city

Caribbean Sea

Angel Falls

Panama Canal

Caracas

Orinoco

River

Bogotá

VENEZUELA

COLOMBIA

N
W E
S

Equator

Quito

ECUADOR

River Amazon

Amazon Rainforest

GALAPAGOS ISLANDS

Andes Mountains

PERU

Pacific Ocean

Lima

BOLIVIA

La Paz

Lake Titicaca

Atacama Desert

Giant tortoises
Giant tortoises live on the Galapagos Islands. Some of them are more than 100 years old.

Santiago

ARGENTINA

CHILE

Chile flag

Cape Horn

8

GUYANA
Georgetown
Paramaribo
SURINAME
Cayenne
FRENCH GUIANA

Equator

BRAZIL

River Paraná

Brasilia

PARAGUAY

Asunción

Rio de Janeiro

Atlantic Ocean

URUGUAY

Montevideo
Buenos Aires

FALKLAND ISLANDS

Amazon Indians

Brazil flag

Venezuela flag

Lake Titicaca
Lake Titicaca is high up in the Andes Mountains. The local fishermen use boats made of reeds.

Toucan
Many different animals live in the Amazon Rainforest. Toucans have large, brightly-coloured bills.

Llama

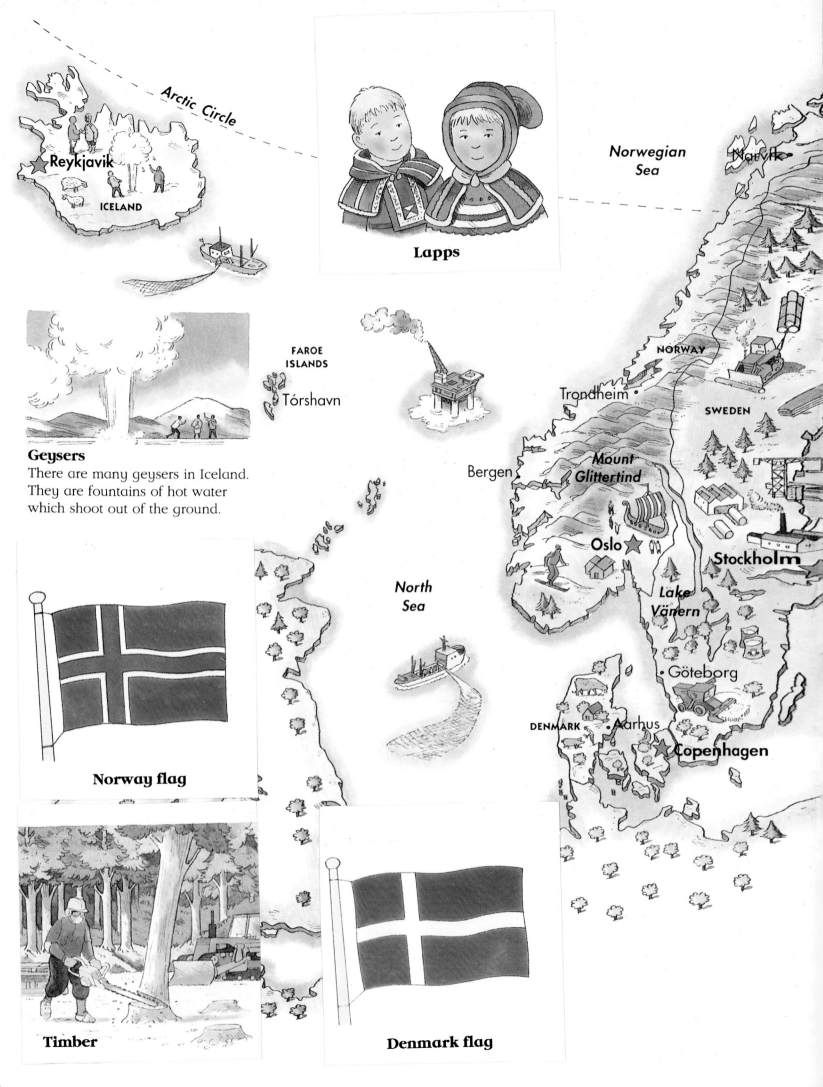

Arctic Circle

Reykjavik

ICELAND

Lapps

Norwegian Sea

Narvik

FAROE ISLANDS

Tórshavn

Geysers

There are many geysers in Iceland. They are fountains of hot water which shoot out of the ground.

NORWAY

Trondheim

SWEDEN

Bergen

Mount Glittertind

North Sea

Oslo

Stockholm

Lake Vänern

Göteborg

Norway flag

DENMARK

Aarhus

Copenhagen

Timber

Denmark flag

Lapland

Oulu

Gulf of Bothnia

FINLAND

. Tampere

★ Helsinki

Baltic
Sea

Midnight sun
The sun never sets in summer in
the north of Scandinavia. But in
winter it stays dark all day long.

Sweden flag

Skiing
It often snows in Scandinavia. In
the countryside it is easier to ski
than walk.

Scandinavia

Scandinavia is in the north
of Europe. It is made up
of Sweden, Denmark,
Norway, Finland and
Iceland. There are lots of
lakes and forests in
Scandinavia. There are
mountains in Sweden and
Norway and volcanoes in
Iceland. The north of
Scandinavia is in the Arctic
Circle where it is very cold
all year round.

This is where
Scandinavia
is on the
globe.

When the time in
London is 9 o'clock
in the morning…

…it is 10 o'clock in the
morning in Stockholm,
Sweden.

KEY TO SYMBOLS USED	
	Mountains
	Forests
	Ice and snow
	Tundra
★	Capital city

West Europe

Some of the richest countries in the world are in West Europe. There are many towns and cities. They have lots of factories and industries. There are many farms in the countryside. France is the biggest country in West Europe. The Vatican City in Rome, Italy, is the smallest. Twelve of the countries make up the European Community.

This is where West Europe is on the globe.

When the time in London is 9 o'clock in the morning…

…it is 10 o'clock in the morning in Rome, Italy.

KEY TO SYMBOLS USED

Mountains	Mountains
Forests	Forests
Capital city	Capital city

United Kingdom flag

France flag

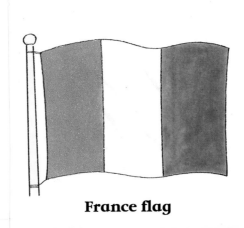

Europort
Rotterdam in the Netherlands is the biggest port in the world. Its quayside is over 100 kilometres long (62 miles).

Flamenco
Flamenco is a style of music and dancing in Spain. Dancers wear colourful costumes and musicians play guitars.

IRELAND

Dublin

Atlantic Ocean

Bay of Biscay

PORTUGAL

River Tagus

Lisbon

Madrid

SPAIN

Seville

GIBRALTAR

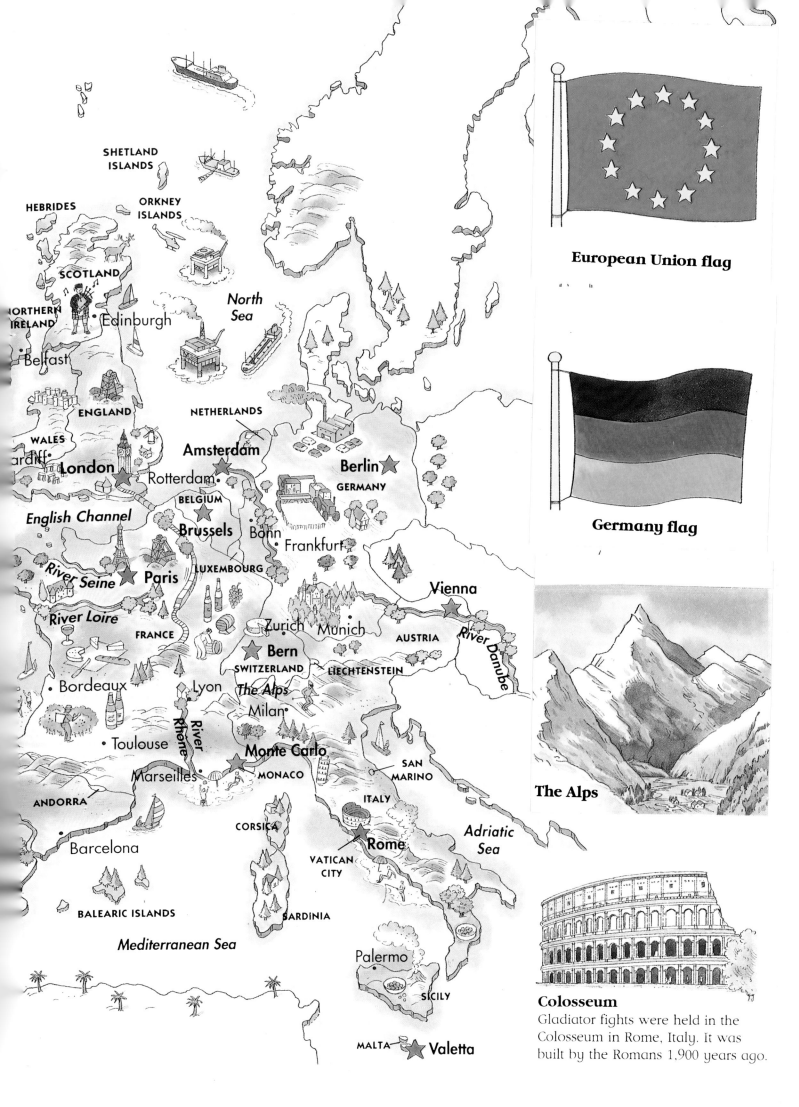

SHETLAND
ISLANDS

HEBRIDES

ORKNEY
ISLANDS

SCOTLAND

NORTHERN
IRELAND · Edinburgh

North
Sea

· Belfast

ENGLAND

WALES

Cardiff · London

Rotterdam ·

Amsterdam

NETHERLANDS

Berlin

GERMANY

English Channel

BELGIUM

Bonn ·

Brussels

· Frankfurt

LUXEMBOURG

River Seine

Paris

Vienna

River Loire

Zurich

Munich

AUSTRIA

River Danube

FRANCE

Bern

SWITZERLAND

LIECHTENSTEIN

· Bordeaux

Lyon ·

The Alps

Milan ·

River Rhône

· Toulouse

Monte Carlo

Marseilles

MONACO

SAN
MARINO

ANDORRA

· Barcelona

CORSICA

ITALY

Adriatic
Sea

VATICAN
CITY

Rome

BALEARIC ISLANDS

SARDINIA

Mediterranean Sea

Palermo

SICILY

MALTA Valetta

European Union flag

Germany flag

The Alps

Colosseum
Gladiator fights were held in the
Colosseum in Rome, Italy. It was
built by the Romans 1,900 years ago.

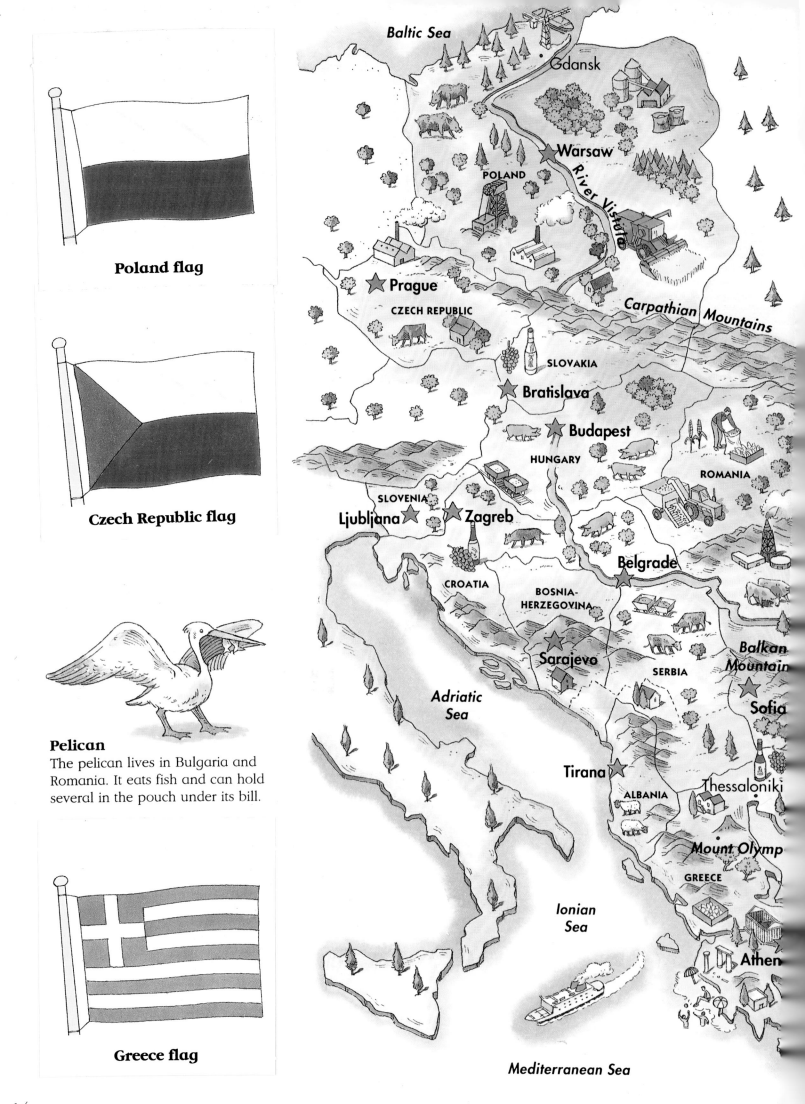

Poland flag

Czech Republic flag

Pelican

The pelican lives in Bulgaria and Romania. It eats fish and can hold several in the pouch under its bill.

Greece flag

Baltic Sea

Gdansk

Warsaw

POLAND

River Vistula

Prague

CZECH REPUBLIC

Carpathian Mountains

SLOVAKIA

Bratislava

Budapest

HUNGARY

ROMANIA

SLOVENIA

Ljubljana

Zagreb

Belgrade

CROATIA

BOSNIA-HERZEGOVINA

Sarajevo

SERBIA

Balkan Mountain

Sofia

Adriatic Sea

Tirana

ALBANIA

Thessaloniki

Mount Olymp

GREECE

Ionian Sea

Athen

Mediterranean Sea

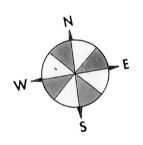

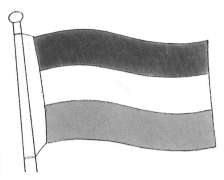

Hungary flag

Carpathian Mountains
This high mountain range crosses Romania. The mountain slopes are covered in thick forest.

Bucharest

River Danube

BULGARIA

Black Sea

TURKEY (part of)

Aegean Sea

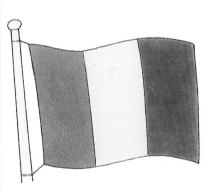

Romania flag

RHODES

CRETE

Crete
Thousands of years ago people on the island of Crete jumped over bulls for sport.

East and South Europe

East Europe stretches from the cold Baltic Sea in the north to the warm Mediterranean Sea in the south. Some countries in East Europe have thick forests where wild animals live. The countries in the north have lots of industries. The south is much warmer and is popular with holiday-makers.

This is where East and South Europe are on the globe.

When the time in London is 9 o'clock in the morning…

…it is 11 o'clock in the morning in Sofia, Bulgaria.

KEY TO SYMBOLS USED	
Mountains	
Forests	
Capital city	

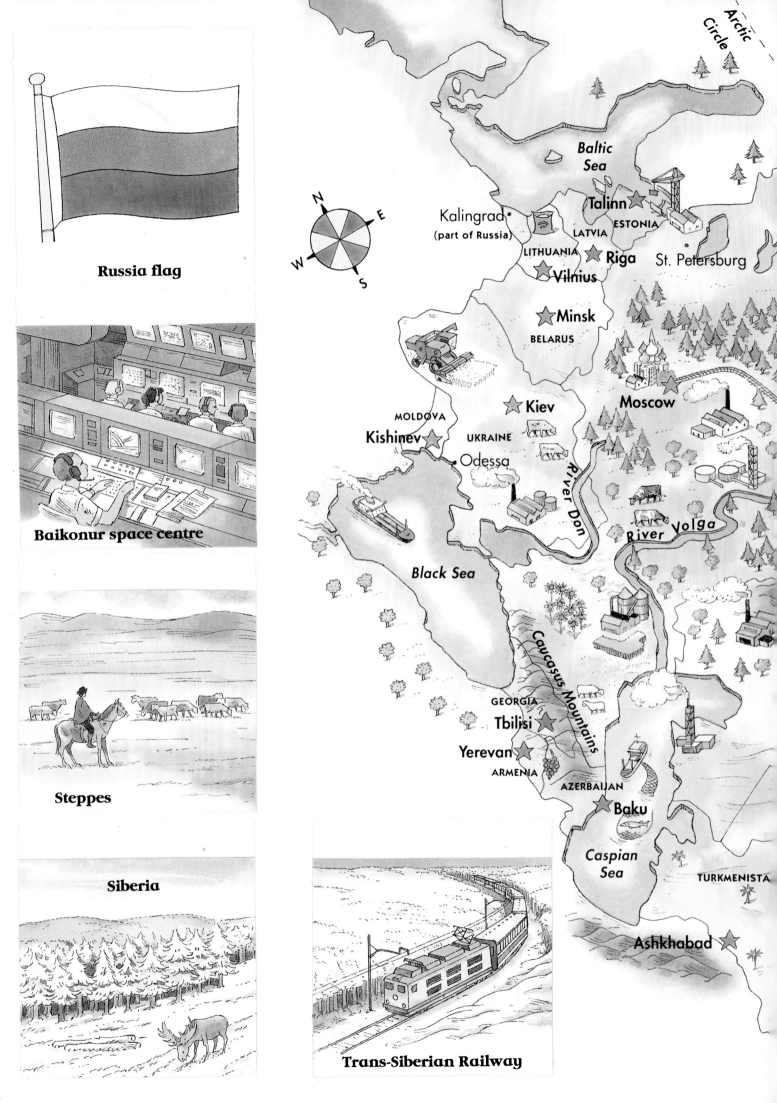

Russia flag

Baikonur space centre

Steppes

Siberia

Trans-Siberian Railway

Arctic Circle

Baltic Sea

Talinn

ESTONIA

Kalingrad
(part of Russia)

LATVIA

LITHUANIA

Riga

St. Petersburg

Vilnius

Minsk

BELARUS

Moscow

MOLDOVA

Kiev

Kishinev

UKRAINE

Odessa

River Don

River Volga

Black Sea

Caucasus Mountains

GEORGIA

Tbilisi

Yerevan

ARMENIA

AZERBAIJAN

Baku

Caspian Sea

TURKMENISTA

Ashkhabad

Barents Sea

• Murmansk

St. Basil's Cathedral

This cathedral is in Moscow. Its domes are shaped like onions. It is 450 years old.

Archangelsk

RUSSIA

Siberia

Trans-Siberian Railway

Ural Mountains

River Ob

Tomsk

• Omsk

River Irtysh

Altai Mountains

Baikonur space centre

Karaganda

Aral Sea

KAZAKHSTAN

steppes

UZBEKISTAN

Tashkent

Samarkand

Frunze

Alma-Ata

KYRGYZSTAN

Dushanbe

TAJIKISTAN

Commonwealth of Independent States (the CIS)

The CIS is made up of most of the states that used to belong to the old Soviet Union. Russia is the largest state in the CIS and is the largest country in the world. Most people live in the west of the CIS, which is in Europe. Only a few people live in the east, which is in Asia.

This is where the CIS is on the globe.

When the time in London is 9 o'clock in the morning…

…it is 12 o'clock in the morning in Moscow, Russia.

KEY TO SYMBOLS USED	
⌒⌒⌒	Mountains
🌲🌲🌲	Forests
～～	Deserts
～～	Tundra
⭐	Capital city

17

Africa

Africa is the second largest continent, after Asia. It contains over 50 countries. In the north there is a huge desert called the Sahara Desert. Further south are forests and grasslands where animals such as giraffes and elephants live. The River Nile is the longest river in the world. It is 6,741 kilometres long (4,187 miles).

This is where Africa is on the globe.

When the time in London is 9 o'clock in the morning...

...it is 10 o'clock in the morning in Kinshasa, Zaïre.

KEY TO SYMBOLS USED	
⛰	Mountains
〰	Deserts
⋯	Grasslands
🌴	Tropical forests
★	Capital city

Sahara Desert
The Sahara Desert covers much of northern Africa. It is the largest desert in the world.

Ghana flag

Zaïre flag

Giraffes
Giraffes live in the grasslands in the middle of Africa. They are the tallest animals in the world.

Rabat
MOROCCO
CANARY ISLANDS
Atlas Mountains
El Aiun
WESTERN SAHARA
MAURITANIA
MALI
Nouakchott
SENEGAL
River Niger
Dakar
GAMBIA
Bamako
BURKINA FASO
GUINEA-BISSAU
GHANA
GUINEA
IVORY COAST
BENIN
Conakry
TOGO
SIERRA LEONE
Monrovia
LIBERIA
Abidjan
Accra

Equator

Atlantic Ocean

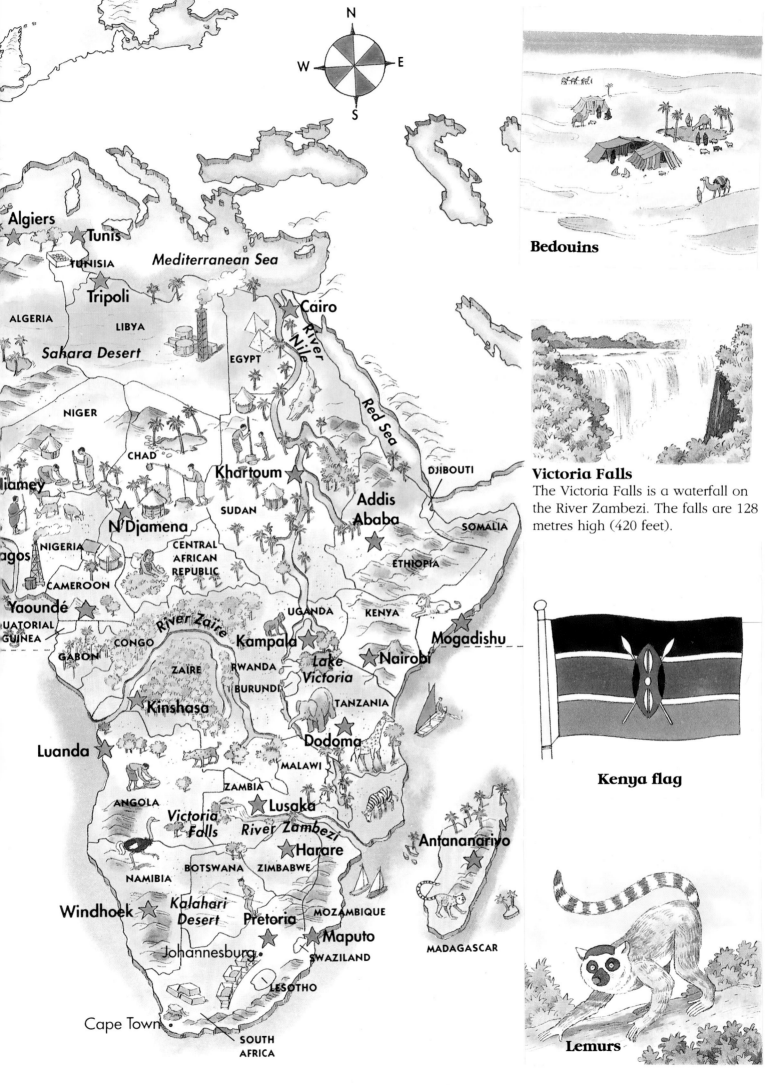

N
W E
S

Algiers
Tunis
TUNISIA
Mediterranean Sea
Tripoli
ALGERIA
LIBYA
Sahara Desert
EGYPT
River Nile
Cairo
Red Sea

NIGER
CHAD
Khartoum
SUDAN
Addis Ababa
DJIBOUTI
SOMALIA
ETHIOPIA

Djamey
N'Djamena
NIGERIA
CENTRAL AFRICAN REPUBLIC
CAMEROON
Lagos
Yaoundé
EQUATORIAL GUINEA
GABON
CONGO
River Zaire
ZAIRE
Kampala
UGANDA
RWANDA
BURUNDI
Lake Victoria
KENYA
Nairobi
Mogadishu

Kinshasa
TANZANIA
Dodoma
Luanda
MALAWI
ANGOLA
ZAMBIA
Victoria Falls
Lusaka
River Zambezi
Harare
BOTSWANA
ZIMBABWE
NAMIBIA
Windhoek
Kalahari Desert
MOZAMBIQUE
Antananarivo
Pretoria
Maputo
Johannesburg
SWAZILAND
MADAGASCAR
LESOTHO
Cape Town
SOUTH AFRICA

Bedouins

Victoria Falls
The Victoria Falls is a waterfall on the River Zambezi. The falls are 128 metres high (420 feet).

Kenya flag

Lemurs

19

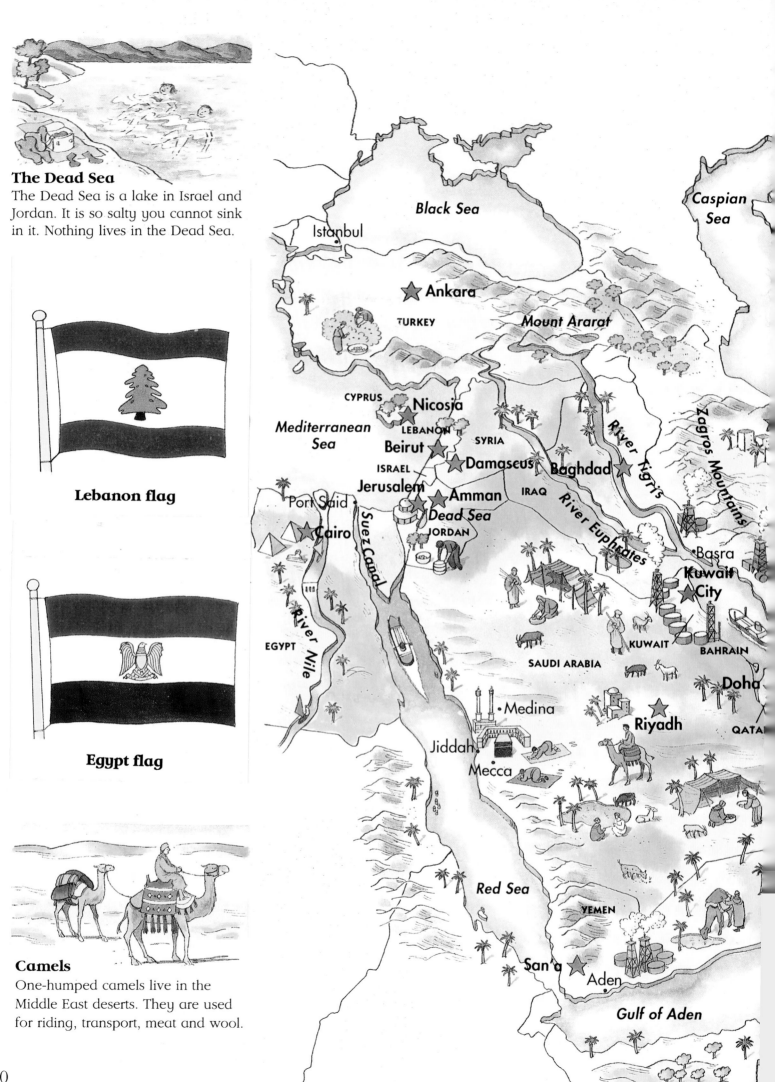

The Dead Sea

The Dead Sea is a lake in Israel and Jordan. It is so salty you cannot sink in it. Nothing lives in the Dead Sea.

Lebanon flag

Egypt flag

Camels

One-humped camels live in the Middle East deserts. They are used for riding, transport, meat and wool.

Black Sea

Caspian Sea

Istanbul

★ Ankara

TURKEY

Mount Ararat

CYPRUS

★ Nicosia

LEBANON

Mediterranean Sea

★ Beirut

★ Damascus

SYRIA

★ Baghdad

River Tigris

Zagros Mountains

ISRAEL

Jerusalem

★ Amman

Dead Sea

IRAQ

River Euphrates

Port Said

Cairo

Suez Canal

JORDAN

Basra

Kuwait City

EGYPT

River Nile

KUWAIT

BAHRAIN

SAUDI ARABIA

Doha

Medina

Riyadh

QATAR

Jiddah

Mecca

Red Sea

YEMEN

San'a

Aden

Gulf of Aden

20

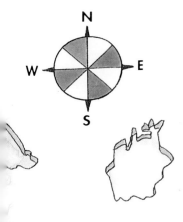

Tehran

IRAN

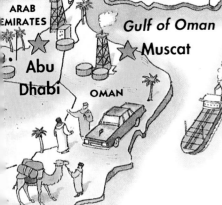

UNITED
ARAB
EMIRATES

Gulf of Oman

Muscat

Abu
Dhabi

OMAN

Arabian Sea

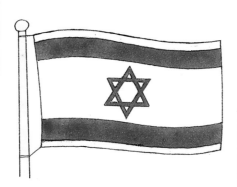

Israel flag

Oil

Saudi Arabia flag

Arab sheikhs
Most people in the Middle East are
Arabs. Long robes keep them cool.
An Arab leader is called a sheikh.

The Middle East

The Middle East is where
Africa, Asia and Europe
meet. Most of the Middle
East is very hot, but it can
get cold in the mountains in
winter. Some of the countries
in the Middle East are rich
because lots of oil has been
found in them. Religion is
important to the people of
the Middle East. There are
many holy places where
people go to worship.

This is where the
Middle East is
on the
globe.

When the time in
London is 9 o'clock
in the morning…

…it is 12 o'clock in the
afternoon in Riyadh,
Saudi Arabia.

KEY TO SYMBOLS USED	
⌒⌒⌒	Mountains
◡◡	Deserts
▱	Grassland
★	Capital city

21

India and its neighbours

India and its neighbours make up an area called South Asia. This area includes India, Pakistan, Bangladesh, Sri Lanka, Afghanistan, Nepal, Myanmar (Burma) and the tiny kingdoms of Bhutan and Sikkim. About one fifth of all the people in the world live in South Asia. Many of them live by farming and growing crops such as rice.

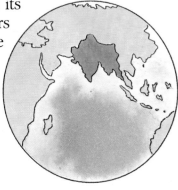

This is where India and its neighbours are on the globe.

When the time in London is 9 o'clock in the morning…

…it is half past two in the afternoon in Delhi, India.

KEY TO SYMBOLS USED

	Mountains
	Deserts
	Tropical forests
★	Capital city

India flag

Pakistan flag

Indian elephant

Tea picking
More tea is grown in India than anywhere else in the world. The young leaves are picked by hand.

Kabul ★

AFGHANISTAN

PAKISTAN

River Indus

• Karachi

Arabian Sea

LAKSHADWEEP ISLANDS

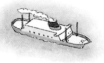

MALDIVE ISLANDS

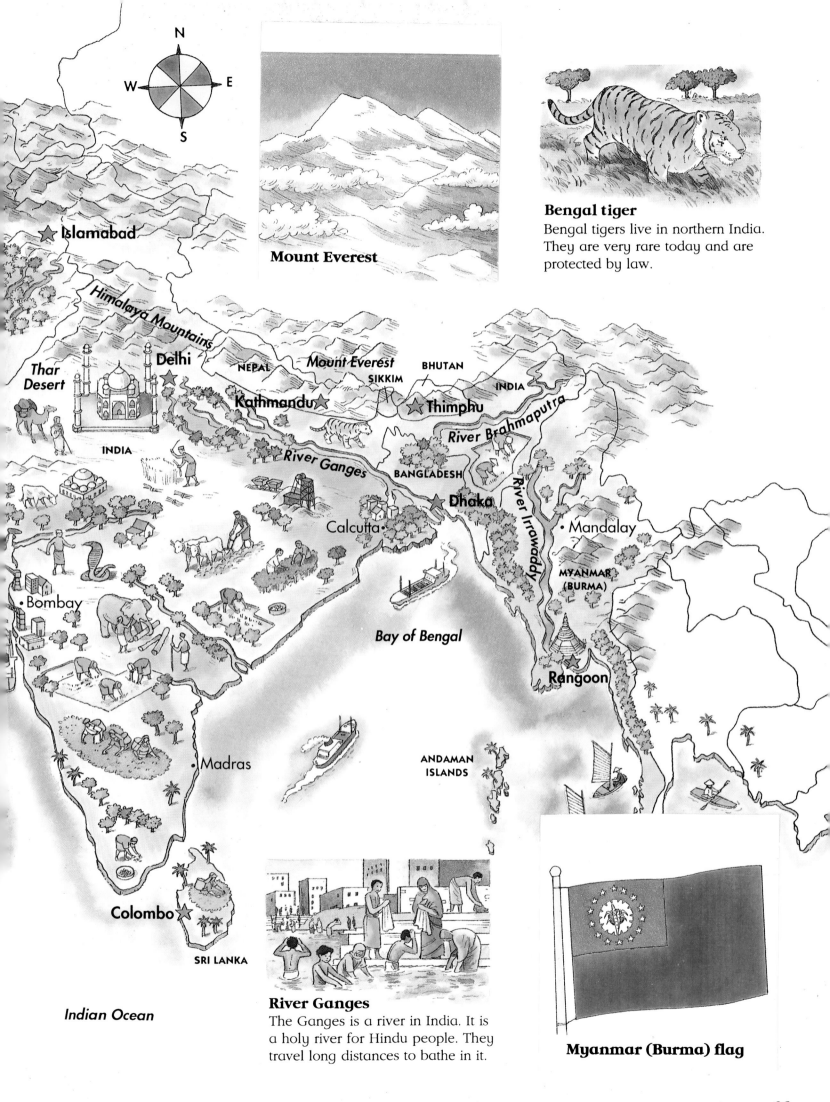

Mount Everest

Bengal tiger
Bengal tigers live in northern India. They are very rare today and are protected by law.

N
W E
S

Islamabad

Himalaya Mountains

Thar Desert

Delhi
NEPAL
Mount Everest
BHUTAN
SIKKIM
INDIA

Kathmandu
Thimphu

River Brahmaputra

INDIA

River Ganges
BANGLADESH

Dhaka

Calcutta

River Irrawaddy

• Mandalay

• Bombay

MYANMAR (BURMA)

Bay of Bengal

Rangoon

• Madras

ANDAMAN ISLANDS

Colombo

SRI LANKA

Indian Ocean

River Ganges
The Ganges is a river in India. It is a holy river for Hindu people. They travel long distances to bathe in it.

Myanmar (Burma) flag

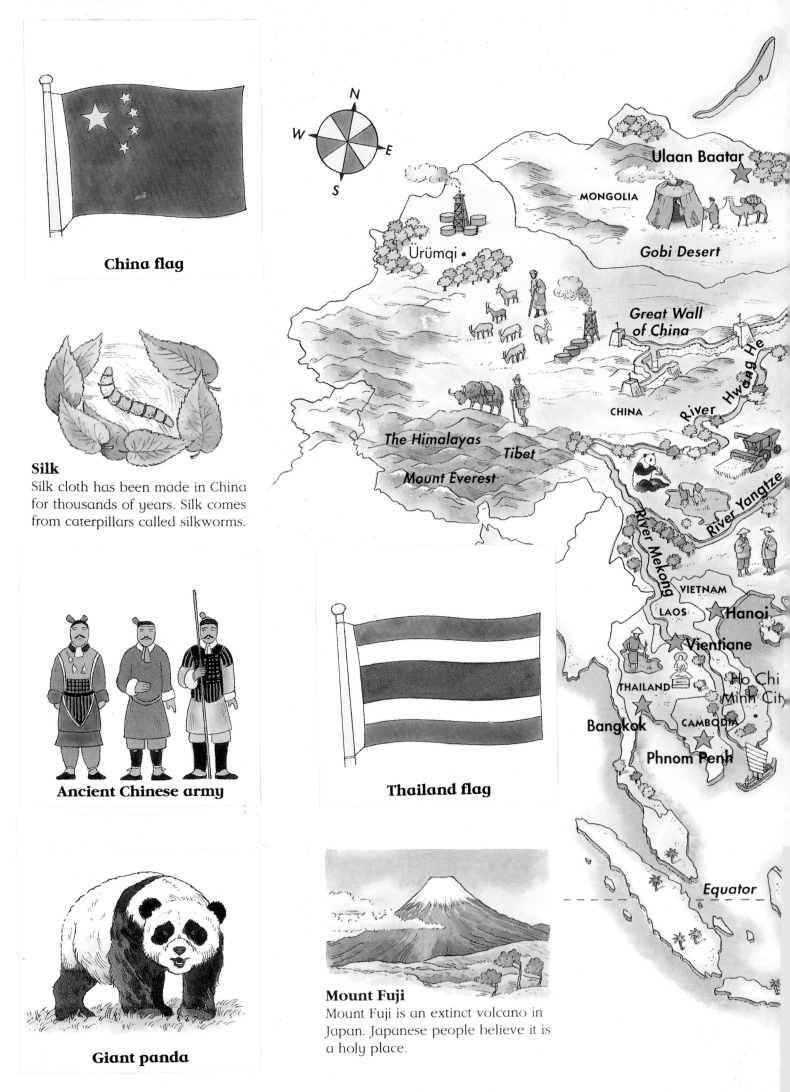

China flag

Silk
Silk cloth has been made in China for thousands of years. Silk comes from caterpillars called silkworms.

Ancient Chinese army

Thailand flag

Giant panda

Mount Fuji
Mount Fuji is an extinct volcano in Japan. Japanese people believe it is a holy place.

N
W   E
S

Ulaan Baatar
MONGOLIA
Gobi Desert
Ürümqi •
Great Wall of China
River Hwang He
CHINA
River Yangtze
The Himalayas
Tibet
Mount Everest
River Mekong
VIETNAM
LAOS
Hanoi
Vientiane
THAILAND
Ho Chi Minh City
Bangkok
CAMBODIA
Phnom Penh
Equator

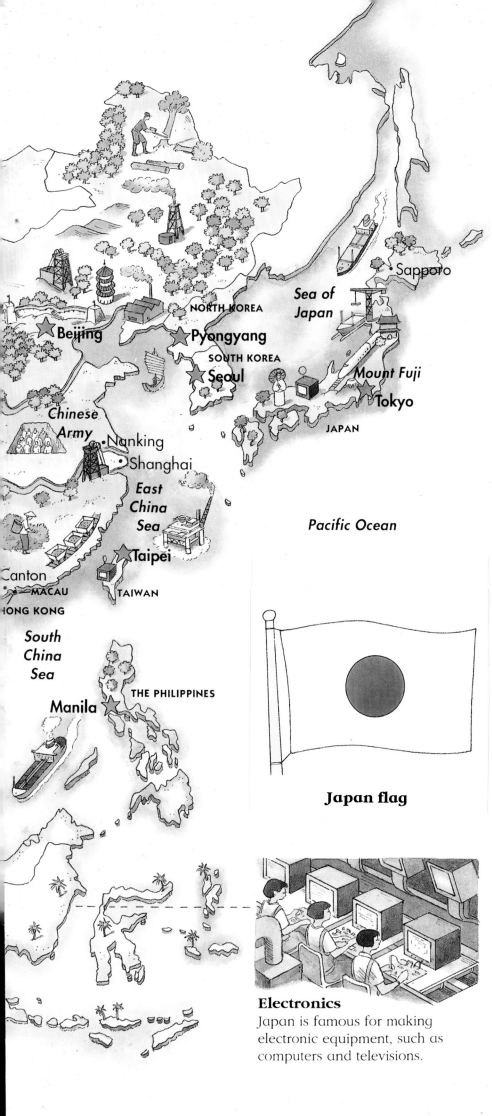

NORTH KOREA

Sea of
Japan

Sapporo

Beijing

Pyongyang

SOUTH KOREA

Seoul

Mount Fuji

*Chinese
Army*

Tokyo

•Nanking

JAPAN

•Shanghai

*East
China
Sea*

Pacific Ocean

Taipei

Canton

MACAU

TAIWAN

HONG KONG

*South
China
Sea*

THE PHILIPPINES

Manila

Japan flag

Electronics
Japan is famous for making
electronic equipment, such as
computers and televisions.

China and its neighbours

China and the countries around it are in the east of Asia. Nearly one quarter of all the people in the world live in China. There are mountains in the west of China and deserts in the north. The countries to the south of China are hot and have jungles. Japan is made up of lots of islands.

This is where China and its neighbours are on the globe.

When the time in London is 9 o'clock in the morning…

…it is 5 o'clock in the afternoon in Beijing, China.

KEY TO SYMBOLS USED	
⌒⌒	Mountains
🌳🌳🌳	Forests
⌒	Deserts
★	Capital city

Australia and South East Asia

Australia is the world's smallest continent. Together with New Zealand, New Guinea and the islands of Indonesia and the Pacific Ocean this huge area is called Australasia. New Guinea is the second largest island in the world – Greenland is the largest.

South East Asia is made up of a small piece of mainland and thousands of tropical islands.

This is where Australia and South East Asia are on the globe.

When the time in London is 9 o'clock in the morning…

…it is 7 o'clock in the evening in Sydney, Australia.

KEY TO SYMBOLS USED	
Mountains	
Deserts	
Grassland	
Tropical forests	
Capital city	

MALAYSIA
BRUNEI
Bandar Seri Begawan
Kuala Lumpur
SARAWAK
Singapore
SUMATRA
BORNEO
SULAWESI
Java Sea
INDONESIA
Jakarta
JAVA

Orang-utan

Indian Ocean

Rubber tapping
Rubber comes from South East Asia. Slits are cut in rubber trees and the rubbery sap is collected in bowls.

Perth

Australia flag

Sydney Opera House
This building is in Sydney, Australia. It is used for music concerts and theatre plays.

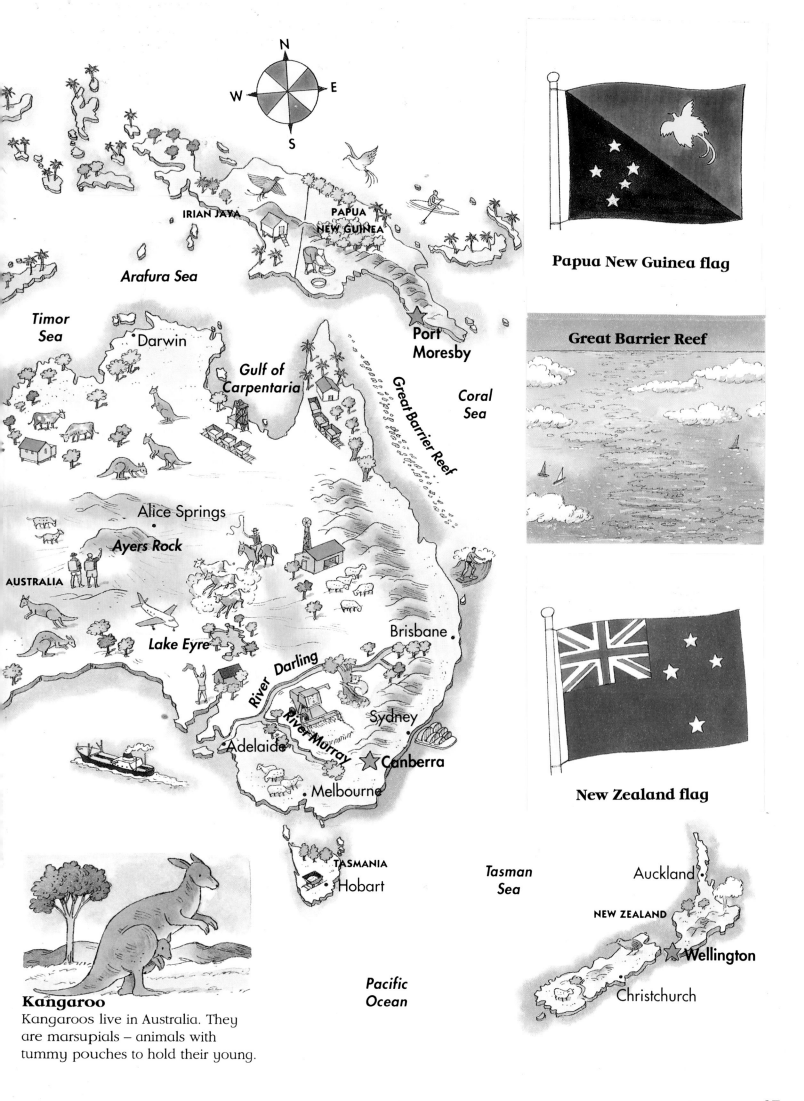

Papua New Guinea flag

Great Barrier Reef

New Zealand flag

IRIAN JAYA

PAPUA NEW GUINEA

Arafura Sea

Timor Sea

Darwin

Gulf of Carpentaria

Port Moresby

Coral Sea

Great Barrier Reef

Alice Springs

Ayers Rock

AUSTRALIA

Lake Eyre

Brisbane

River Darling

River Murray

Sydney

Adelaide

⭐ **Canberra**

Melbourne

TASMANIA

Hobart

Tasman Sea

Auckland

NEW ZEALAND

⭐ **Wellington**

Christchurch

Pacific Ocean

Kangaroo
Kangaroos live in Australia. They are marsupials – animals with tummy pouches to hold their young.

The Arctic and the Antarctic

The Arctic and the Antarctic are huge cold areas of ice and snow. The Arctic is in the far north. There is no land there, but the sea is always frozen. The Antarctic is in the far south. Its land is covered in a thick sheet of ice. Only a few people live in the Arctic and the Antarctic.

Arctic

This is where the Arctic and the Antarctic are on the globe.

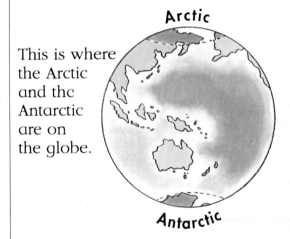

Antarctic

The average January temperature in the Arctic is 40°C below freezing point. In July it is 0°C.

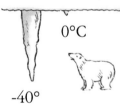

0°C

-40°

The average January temperature in the Antarctic is 25°C below freezing point. In July it is 50°C below freezing point.

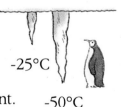

-25°C

-50°C

KEY TO SYMBOLS USED

 Mountains

 Ice and snow

Tundra

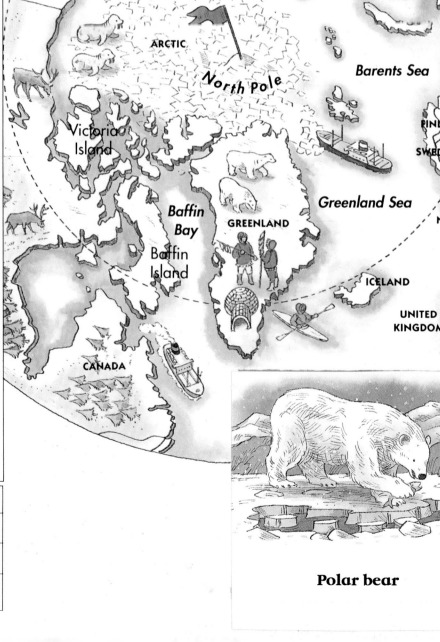

Inuit

Arctic Circle

Bering Strait

RUSSIA

Arctic Ocean

UNITED STATES (Alaska)

ARCTIC

North Pole

Barents Sea

Victoria Island

FINLAND

SWEDEN

Greenland Sea

NORWAY

Baffin Bay

GREENLAND

Baffin Island

ICELAND

UNITED KINGDOM

CANADA

Polar bear

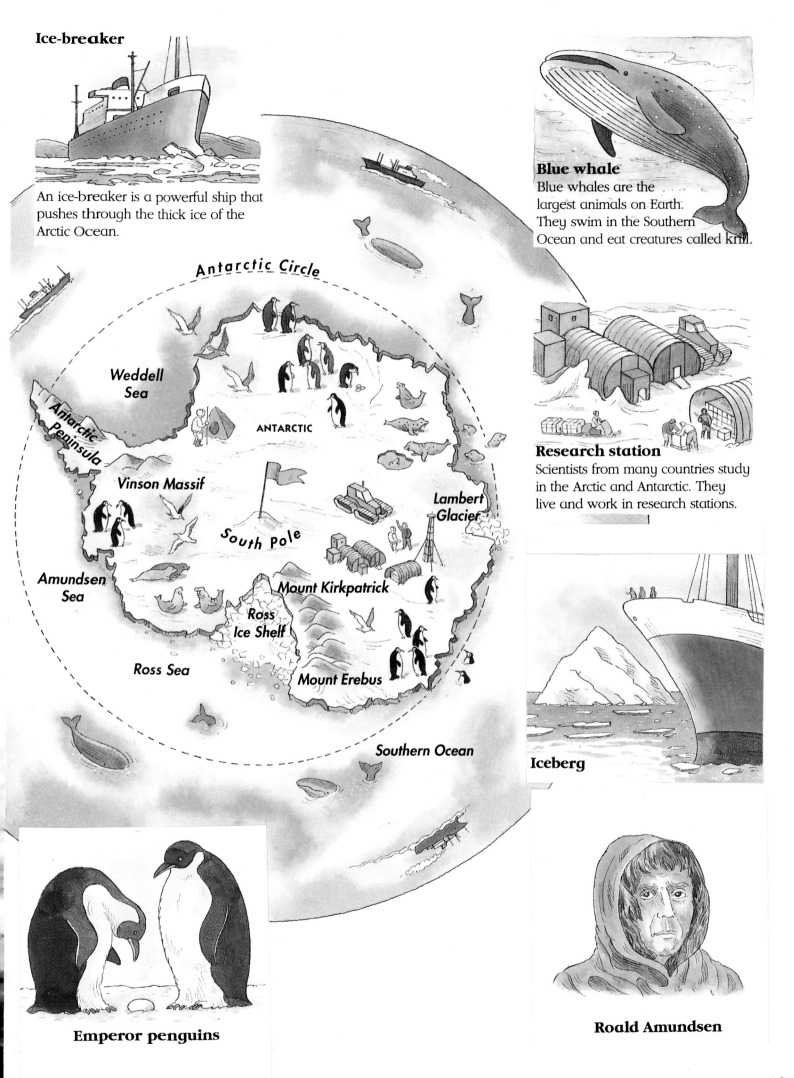

Ice-breaker

An ice-breaker is a powerful ship that pushes through the thick ice of the Arctic Ocean.

Blue whale

Blue whales are the largest animals on Earth. They swim in the Southern Ocean and eat creatures called krill.

Research station

Scientists from many countries study in the Arctic and Antarctic. They live and work in research stations.

Antarctic Circle

Weddell Sea

Antarctic Peninsula

ANTARCTIC

Vinson Massif

Lambert Glacier

South Pole

Amundsen Sea

Mount Kirkpatrick

Ross Ice Shelf

Mount Erebus

Ross Sea

Southern Ocean

Iceberg

Emperor penguins

Roald Amundsen

THE

NORTH
AMERICA

WEST
EUROPE

TROPIC OF CANCER

CENTRAL
AMERICA

EQUATOR

SOUTH
AMERICA

NORTH

WEST   EAST

SOUTH